09709

KU-288-521

The Water Cycle

Jen Green

WAYLAND

First published in 2007 by Wayland
Reprinted in 2007
Copyright © Wayland 2007

Wayland
338 Euston Road
London NW1 3BH

Wayland Australia
Level 17/207 Kent Street
Sydney NSW 2000

Produced by Tall Tree Ltd
Editor: Jon Richards
Designer: Ben Ruocco
Consultant: John Williams

Green, Jen
    The water cycle. – (Our Earth)
    1. Hydrologic cycle – Juvenile literature
    I. Title
    551.4'8

    ISBN-13: 9780750250085

Printed in China
Wayland is a division of Hachette
Children's Books, a Hachette Livre
UK Company

Contents

Water everywhere

Water is all around us, flowing in seas, lakes and rivers. It pours from the sky and collects in puddles. Air, plants, soil and rocks contain water.

◆ Water has hundreds of uses, for drinking, farming, energy and transport. We have fun in water too!

Water covers over 70 per cent of the Earth's surface.

Fact

Almost two-thirds of your body is made from water.

People and animals also contain water. All living things need water for life. Water is so useful that cities, towns and villages are all found near water.

Watery world

Water is found in three forms. As a solid, it is called ice. As a liquid, it is called water. As a gas, it is called **water vapour**. Liquid water is the most common form.

⬇ The Pacific Ocean is the largest ocean, covering a third of Earth's surface.

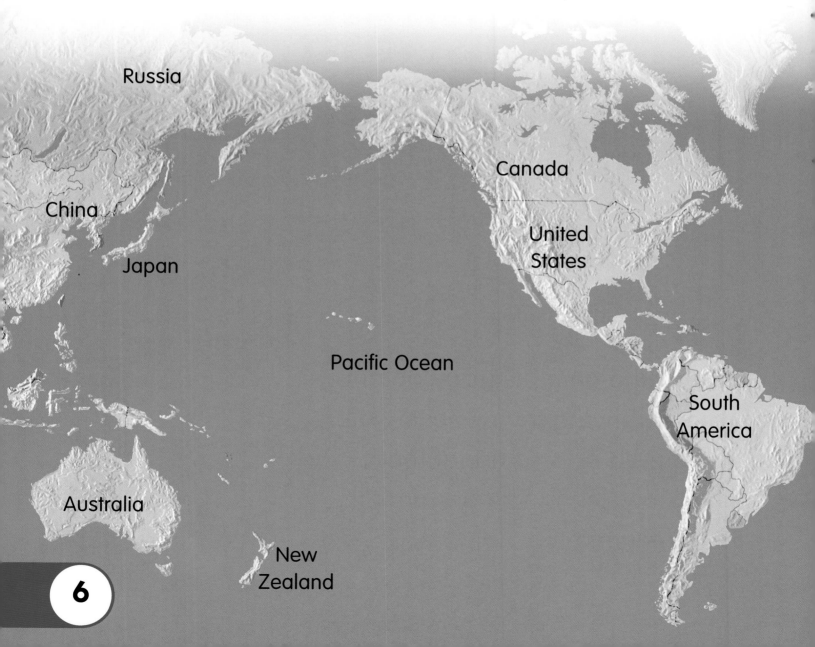

Russia

Canada

China

United States

Japan

Pacific Ocean

South America

Australia

New Zealand

Fact

The Earth looks blue from space because of all the ocean water.

▲ Rivers carry **fresh water** towards the sea.

Dips in the Earth's surface fill with water to form seas and lakes. About 97 per cent of the world's water is salty. Fresh water is found in rivers, lakes, wetlands and frozen ice at the Earth's poles.

Ice

When water gets colder than 0°C (32°F) it freezes to form solid ice. Ice is found in frozen lakes and **glaciers** high on mountains. It covers the land around the Earth's poles and floats on the sea as icebergs.

⬇ Ice is lighter than water, so it floats.

The land around the South Pole is covered by an **ice cap** that is up to 3 km (2 miles) thick. The ice here contains 90 per cent of the world's fresh water.

⬇ The ice in a glacier flows very slowly downhill.

Fact

Nine-tenths of an iceberg lies below the water's surface.

Water as a gas

All air contains some water vapour. When you breathe out, your breath contains water vapour. If you breathe on a mirror, tiny drops of water appear on the glass.

▶▶ **Geysers** are natural fountains that spout steam and hot water. The water is heated by hot rocks underground.

⌄ Steam rises from a pan of boiling water. You can cook vegetables in the hot steam.

Fact

A geyser called Old Faithful in North America spouts water and steam every 60 to 70 minutes.

When water is heated to 100°C (212°F), it turns into a hot gas called **steam**. You can see steam rising from water when a kettle is boiled.

The water cycle

In the **water cycle**, water changes from a gas to a liquid to a solid and back as it moves between the air, land and oceans.

⬇ Drops of water in the air join together to form clouds.

Water rises from seas, lakes and puddles as water vapour. As the water vapour rises, it is cooled by the cold air higher up. As it cools, water droplets gather together to form clouds.

⊻ The air around the tops of mountains is cold and clouds can form here.

From clouds to rain

The water in clouds falls as rain. Inside clouds, water droplets crash into one another. They join to make bigger droplets. In the end, the droplets get so heavy that they fall as rain.

A short fall of rain is called a shower.

Hailstones may be smaller than peas or bigger than golfballs.

Hailstones are **pellets** of ice. Hail may fall from cold clouds instead of rain. As ice **crystals** get blown about inside clouds, they are coated with more ice. They get heavy and crash to the ground.

15

From rivers to the sea

When rain falls, the water flows over the ground or through the soil and into streams. Streams flow into rivers that empty into the sea or a lake.

A waterfall forms where rushing water carves a step in the rock.

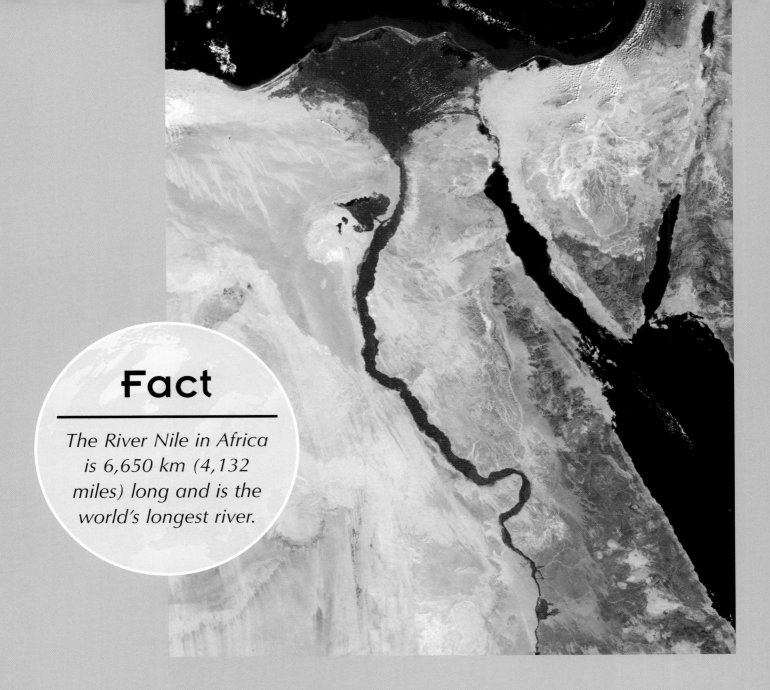

As a river moves towards the sea it flows over waterfalls and winds its way through the land. Where it meets the sea, the river may form a **delta**. When the water reaches the sea, the water cycle starts again.

The delta of the River Nile in Africa is the large green triangle at the top of this photo. This flat land has formed where the river meets the sea.

Underground water

After rain falls, water soaks into the ground. It trickles down through the soil and can collect in the rocks below. Water flowing underground can carve caves into soft rock.

❯❯ A big tree can draw hundreds of litres of water in a day from the soil and into its trunk, branches and leaves.

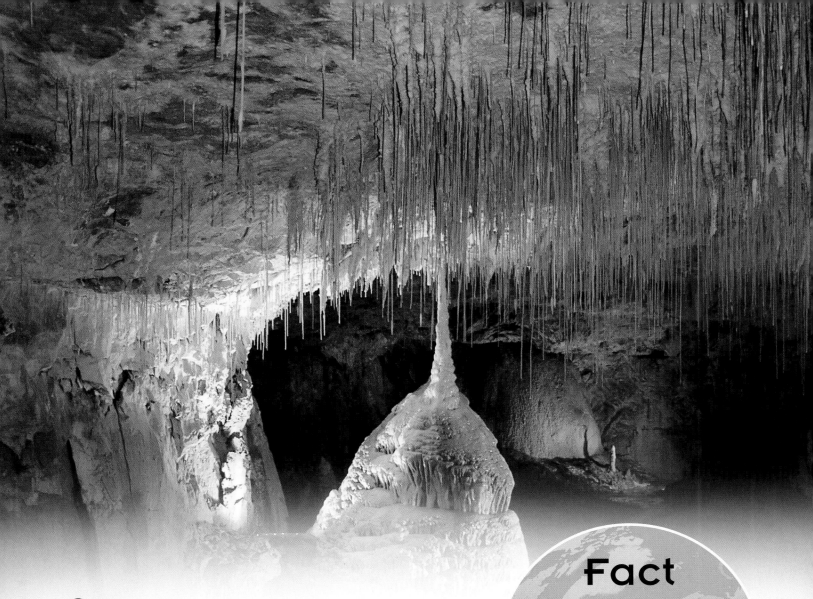

▲ Water has worn away this rock, called limestone, to make a large cave.

Plants use their roots to draw water up from the soil. They use this water to grow. Any unused water leaves the plant as water vapour. It passes out through the leaves and into the air to start the water cycle again.

Wet and dry

Some parts of the world are wetter than others. Too much rain can cause a **flood**. Water spills over the banks of a river and covers the land.

⊗ Flooding can cause damage to homes and property.

⬢ Drought has caused the dry ground to crack.

Too little rain falling in a region is called a **drought**. Deserts are places where hardly any rain falls. Life in these regions is very difficult because water is so important to plants and animals.

Activities

Collecting water from the air

Warm air may contain lots of water.
Find out how you can collect this
water with this simple project.

WHAT YOU NEED

- **Large bowl**
- **Cup**
- **Cling film**
- **Pebble**
- **Warm water**

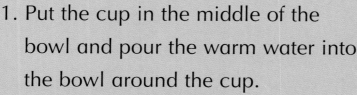

1. Put the cup in the middle of the
   bowl and pour the warm water into
   the bowl around the cup.
2. Cover the top of the bowl with cling
   film. Place the pebble in the
   middle of the cling film.
3. After a few minutes you
   will see water droplets
   form on the cling film
   and collect in the cup.

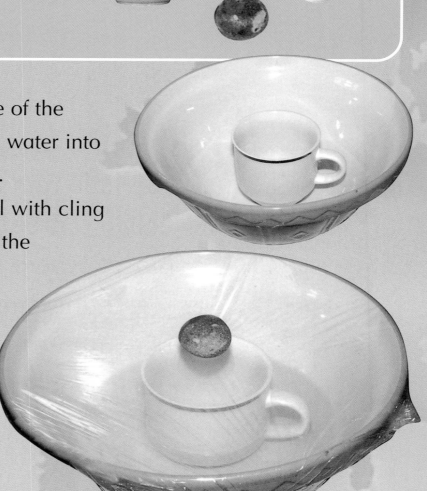

Floating in water

This project will show you one of the main differences between **saltwater** and fresh water.

1. Pour some water into the two cups.
2. Add salt to one of the cups and stir until no more salt will dissolve. Stop when you see that some salt remains at the bottom of the cup.
3. Mark dots on each straw at regular intervals. Push a piece of modelling clay onto one end of each straw and then place them in the water.
4. The straw in the saltwater will float higher. This is because the saltwater is thicker, or more dense, and pushes up on the straw.

Glossary

Crystals Solid materials that have flat sides which are set at angles to each other, such as ice.

Delta A marshy area formed where a river meets the sea. The river drops the rocks and soil it was carrying to form the delta.

Droplets Tiny drops.

Drought When little or no rain falls.

Fresh water Water that is not salty.

Flood When water from rivers or the sea overflows and covers the land.

Geysers Openings in the ground that regularly spout steam and hot water.

Glaciers Large bodies of ice that move very slowly. Glaciers are found around the poles and high on the slopes of mountains.

Ice cap A thick sheet of ice. Ice caps cover the regions around the Earth's poles.

Pellets Small, hard lumps.

Saltwater Water that contains salt and minerals.

Steam Water that has been heated until it forms a gas.

Water vapour Water in the form of a gas.

Water cycle The movement of water from a gas to a liquid and back to a gas, as it moves from the air, to rivers, to the sea and back to the air.

Index